Forget the Box 2020

First published in the UK in 2014 by Kate & Stephen Page

Forget the Box – Freeing your imagination to create a stimulating brief
© Kate and Stephen Page

Illustrations
Leaping fox, walking armadillo, sitting fox (p8), sitting bear – Topsell's the history of four-footed beasts and serpents Woodcuts 1658. Special Collections, University of Houston Libraries. University of Houston Digital Library. Web. July 15, 2014. http://digital.lib.uh.edu/collection/p15195coll18

Standing, sitting and sleeping fox, sitting armadillo, standing bear – Sarah Govia

Flamingo, rooster, chameleon, lightening gentlemen – Paul Hunt

Lady (p17), Gentleman (p49) – www.shutterstock.com

Lump Sucker Fish: Select Fables, Memorial edition of Thomas Bewick's works vol. 5
©The Trustees of the British Museum

All other images – http://olddesignshop.com

Quotes
Page 21: How Warren Buffett Avoids Getting Trapped by Confirmation Bias, Forbes Magazine,
          date published May 7 2013, author: Roger Dooley

Page 27: Wonderbook, date published 2013, author: Jeff VanderMeer

Page 37: An Experiment in Criticism, Part of Canto Classics, author: C S Lewis, date published:
          March 2012, Cambridge University Press

CONTENTS

Defining the challenge

- Positioning
- Value proposition

Freeing imaginations

- Why are you doing this?
- Your story and essence
- Winning share-of-mind

Realising ideas

- Creating a communication strategy
- Developing content

We want to free your imaginations so that you and your team don't just think outside the box, you forget the box completely...

Crafting communication

- The creative brief
- What happens next?

FOREWORD

Forget the Box was first published by Kate and Stephen Page in 2014 to help clients engage in the creative process and build inspiring campaigns that make powerful connections with their audiences. It now typifies the approach taken by Page & Page: the multiple award-winning creative communications agency that Kate and Stephen founded. Forget the Box recognises the challenges that time-poor clients and a rapidly changing business environment present, and aims to facilitate a better, more effective briefing process.

At Page & Page the relentless pursuit of creativity is more alive than ever, and the company has one simple aim: to become one of the most influential independently owned creative communications agencies in the world. Breaking down barriers and enabling clients to be part of the creative process is a daily activity at Page & Page. The core value driving the agency revolves around the idea of 'active consideration'. As CS Lewis said, 'The man who is contented to be only himself, and therefore less a self, is in prison. My own eyes are not enough for me, I will see through those of others. Reality, even seen through the eyes of many, is not enough...'

Active consideration means looking out for our fellow team members, it means thinking pro actively about our clients and it means we always seek an insight when we're thinking about target audiences: how can we add value in a way that these people cannot imagine for themselves?

Being actively considerate in everything we do also leads to some truly astonishing business results. A recent campaign enabled one client to increase healthcare professional recruitment by 62%. Another to win an additional 7% market share.

Forget the Box is borne out of tried and tested knowledge, gained through more than 30 years of industry experience. It is designed to facilitate – on hand to offer creative inspiration and guidance to anyone seeking genuinely imaginative and practical solutions.

Only expect a great campaign from
your creative team if you've written
a brief stimulating enough to fire
their imagination...

...this book enables you to
have that expectation!

WE CARRIED OUT
FURTHER RESEARCH...

All marketeers and communicators know that the role insights play in laying the foundations for a good communications strategy is invaluable. Without in-depth knowledge and insight into your audience, there is little hope of challenging the status quo and ultimately changing behaviours. With this in mind, in 2019, we conducted research into the satisfaction levels felt by marketeers and communicators around the world. We stepped outside of our client base and conducted the survey across a wider audience.

Given the importance of and time spent on gathering insights and developing strategies, we wanted to know just how satisfied people were with these two crucial elements of their marketing strategy. So, we took to social media and asked them. This is what they told us:

Almost a quarter (23%) of senior marketeers and communication executives who responded said they were 'dissatisfied' or 'very dissatisfied' with the strategy and the insights that they were using currently. Areas requiring improvement included:

- *Targeting and personalising messages*
- *Reaching beyond the core customer base*
- *Being able to measure success with clear Key Performance Indicators (KPIs)*
- *Understanding customers' motivations*
- *Combining insight with data to improve effectiveness*

66% of senior marketers were 'satisfied' with their strategic approach but only 59% felt the same about their insight. In fact, when we delved deeper into individual responses, we found that 41% respondents felt there was a significant disconnect between how satisfied they were with their strategy versus the insights.

We hope this book goes some way to change this.

FREEING
THE IMAGINATION

It takes imagination to create something meaningful and communicate it well. That process has to start with an inspiring creative brief to give it direction. We understand that writing a brief that inspires is a challenging process – communicating to the creative team everything that needs to be achieved without being too directional and hindering the creative thought process. The right balance can be hard to find. A good brief not only sets out business objectives, potential strategy, and target audience insights, it also, just as importantly, inspires everyone involved.

It can be a daunting task because when writing a brief, you are directly influencing the campaign's potential and the direction it takes. This book, therefore, has two objectives:

- To facilitate collaboration between business-minded people and creative people so that a stimulating brief can be written.
- To help ensure that the brief is clear, informative and has well-defined objectives.

It's a collaborative process
When you use an inclusive process, you're more likely to achieve a stimulating brief resulting in an effective campaign. The input from a variety of people from different backgrounds and job roles working together increases the richness and depth of the ideas. Sharing ideas often then sparks off better ideas that would not have been thought of in isolation.

The exercises in this book are designed to help facilitate that process and bring out the best in everyone there to make a brief that says precisely what you need it to say.

We'll start by showing you the context in which we're working. The way that audiences absorb messaging has changed massively over the last decade, and it's essential to be up to date before we start.

The exercises in this book are not intended to be a fully comprehensive collection of brand building tools (although they will contribute towards the development of a more original brand). It's also not essential to do every task or even to do them in order. Each task has been developed to work in isolation and when combined with others.

Often, the best way to use the exercises is with the help of a facilitator in a group workshop setting. If you do choose to use a facilitator, they need to be someone who fully understands and is experienced in the process. This could be a work colleague, someone from your agency, or someone you source independently. Understandably, smaller-scale projects may not be able to justify the extra cost of a facilitator, but the exercises can still give structure to the thinking, helping to build a better, more inspiring brief.

WHAT AN EFFECTIVE CAMPAIGN COULD DO FOR YOU

Building a successful brand requires imagination

Many successful brands of today, inspire us and fire our imaginations; brands like Soundcloud, Takeda, BMW i, YouTube, Phillips, GSK, Uber, Cook, Seedlip, Prime for instance.

Successful brands achieve this effect because they represent something meaningful. Their messages resonate with their customers and make them feel something. A relationship starts to develop.

This kind of connection can only be created when a powerful insight has been identifyed and acted upon. It is the combination of attracting attention and then offering something valuable in the target audience's mind that makes for a successful brand campaign. The audience falls in love with the brand and then the product. Everyone wants to buy into something they believe in.

What goes on in our heads?

There's one big thing that stands between us humans and a meaningful brand – our brains. If we assume the average person is around 150lb and the average brain weighs 3lb, then this means the brain makes up only 2% of total body weight and in addition to that, no one has an entirely rational mind. Our feelings and instincts drive much of what goes on in our heads.

The physical body is receptive to many sensations: sight, sound, smell, touch and taste. Only a little of this is processed intellectually or rationally. For something to be meaningful, for it to have a chance of reaching the tiny percentage of the body that is rational, it needs first to grab our attention instinctively and intuitively. It needs to fire the imagination in the way enduring brands do. So, we'd argue the point of creativity is not only to grab attention, but also to ensure that the connection between the sender and the receiver of the message feels real.

Bombarded by media

The challenge is magnified by the massive amount of media that bombards us 24 hours a day, 99% of which we instinctively filter out. The influence of instinct and intuition, coupled with all that noise, makes it easy to understand that often only by having creative communication does a brand's stand any chance of success.

WARNING! *While personal (consumer) choices are often made on an instinctive basis, people do sometimes make rational buying decisions. Professional decisions, for example, are usually well thought through. Even in these situations however, we must get beyond the noise in the market place if we are to win attention, and that means igniting our audience's imagination.*

THE RELATIONSHIP BETWEEN BRAND AND AUDIENCE IS CHANGING

When we talk about getting results, we mean creating campaigns that encourage audiences to change their behaviours, attitudes and habits. As the relationship between the brand and the audience continues to change, so a successful briefing process becomes even more vital.

One way of viewing it is that it's more about our customers than it is about us. While in the past we could rely on the uniqueness of an organisation, product or service, now we must work to ensure we fully understand the space our audience is in.

We have to imagine what that target audience would really value most in their space – even if they do not know it themselves. We then set out to create that value. It might be humour, data, a tool, information, a service, something social or something professional, but it must attract their curiosity, over time get them engaged and ultimately pull them into the wider brand experience. Do this extensively and you can take ownership of the space they function within.

The point is this: it is more about them than us.

It's about the audience and the space they're in.

WHAT MAKES A GOOD BRIEF?

The physical evidence will be the smiling faces of the creative team, as their eyes light up. A good brief is based on a new truth or an insight – a leap of imagination pulled from everything learnt about the competition, market dynamics, the target audience and the competitive positioning of the product, service or organisation. That insight is something the creative team can really get their teeth into.

A good brief will be full of conviction – your ideas of how you can add value on behalf of the target audience. You might even call it leadership. Again, this is something that will inspire the creative people.

A good brief is like a signpost at a junction pointing in one direction with complete and utter conviction.

BEING IMAGINATIVE TAKES COURAGE

Active listening makes a difference

It takes courage to offer up ideas. The important thing is to listen to and consider those ideas actively. Not only does this give every idea a chance, but it also gives people more courage to offer those ideas freely.

No idea is perfect right from its conception. To allow an idea to grow into something that could work, there is an exercise that we can practice in "yes, and…". When we say things like "no, but…" we squash any potential that idea may have had and also make others feel invalid should they want to build upon it. In one moment, you take all of the worth away from that idea and, by extension, any further comments on it. By saying things like "yes, and…" it allows the idea to grow organically and be taken in other directions, even if it ends up doing a total 360-degree turn.

It's incredible how quickly the confidence to offer ideas develops among a team when no idea is treated as a bad one or dismissed by participants.

Being original and having inspiration

Innovative ideas don't simply pop into your head because you sit and wait for them. Original thinkers, if they exist, are perhaps the rarest resource on the planet (many would say they are extinct), so don't set out to think of an 'original idea'. It is much better to think in terms of the things you've seen, heard and liked, and imagine how you could apply that to your work. The very act of reinterpreting something transforms it into something new. This is how all creative material be it music, art, entertainment or advertising evolves. Small waves of original thought,

based on previous ideas, result in bigger waves of imaginative ideas. Combine this with the views of your colleagues, and you're on your way to something amazing.

It is more about what you absorb than what you give out

This works best when things around you are stimulating. You need to have been inspired to inspire others. Stimulation can come from anywhere – the key is to be always on the lookout for words, phrases, images, campaigns, art, music, film and other stuff that sparks your imagination. Examples of these things can also be useful to bring into these meetings to help get people going.

We all tend to put on a front to protect ourselves.

Spontaneity

The controlling part of our brain is much less imaginative than our subconscious. We know – we've been in many brainstorms and idea sessions, and often the best ideas surface for no apparent reason in response to something someone just said. One of the best we've encountered was a lady thinking about a campaign for her agency. The agency offered a range of services, and she used the analogy of a food court. She said, "Wouldn't it be good if we could just invite the clients to come in, look around and make their choices?" Her colleagues latched on to this, drawing their own parallels: clients choosing who they wanted to work with at an open day, using a menu of services through a speed dating mechanism. The resulting open day generated a lot of business (the right kind of business).

One of the ways we facilitate productive meetings is with random or vaguely associated objects. We ask everyone at the meeting to tell us, immediately, how they'd use that object to promote the brand. It's spontaneous and can be done just by getting people to look around them. It works even if you are on your own. Everyday objects can be reinterpreted – it is what artists do all the time.

Another fun exercise is to imagine who your brand would be if they were a person: what would the brand's favourite food be? What does the brand do in its spare time? It helps to give the group an idea of the personality that they want to sell people.

Kill your darlings

Arriving at just one good idea is a relief, and we tend to want to hang on to it for dear life. However, the best artists, musicians and writers all 'kill their darlings'. They learn that by returning to a blank sheet of paper after this epiphany, what follows tends to be even better. Why? Well, we're not sure, but it may have something to do with the trains of thought we have now established in our minds. Once we know the pathway, we can figure out how to use it better.

Storytelling and personality

Sometimes being creative is merely retelling the story or revisiting the reason we're promoting the brand in the first place. We let ourselves be led by people who tell the most convincing stories. We might allow them to lead a moment, a meeting, a conversation, a fashion, a team, or a country. Leadership is transient and relevant to a moment, and our ideas can be our story told in the right way at the right time.

All great stories have clearly defined characters and, in the same vein, archetypes (see pages 30–31) give us a human way to relate to a brand and are often used during the brand building process. Each of the 12 archetypes is positioned within four areas: energy, emotion, substance and thought. They help to define the values of a brand.

Cynicism

Never be cynical. It kills the imagination.

WHAT YOU WILL NEED FOR THE EXERCISES

Time

The exercises in this book will take between 30 minutes and 2 hours each, depending on how many people are involved and where your brand is already. Honing and developing the ideas will require additional time; it's never going to be absolutely right the first time. What you produce today will be a springboard tomorrow for even better ideas, because the mind tends to explore ideas subconsciously.

Don't be put off by the amount of time the exercises could take. The important thing is to take the time to get it right; otherwise, you'll end up doing the same task again in six months' time when the work has failed.

Pen and paper

We know that there is nothing as scary as a blank sheet of paper, but there is nothing as immediate as a pen for capturing ideas. Intellect and instinct will come to the forefront to help populate this white space. The more organic the process, the more ideas will surface.

People

Include as many people as you can afford to (within reason) who should and will have a say in the brand. We all see the world differently so the more ideas and insights we can gather from different perspectives, the more productive the result.

Facilitator

It is crucial that someone is there to encourage the quieter stakeholders to speak up and the noisier ones to quieten down.

Attitude

All participants must come with an open mind. People must let their ideas surface. They need to dare to share the thoughts that they might generally keep to themselves. In a workshop, no idea is a bad idea. It's crucial to start with off-the-wall, 'out-there' ideas, and then to rein things back. Don't try and turn something dull into something exciting - it won't work.

Environment

Ideally, the exercises should take place somewhere outside of the office because it helps to release people from their usual thoughts and day-to-day distractions. If you do have to hold the exercises in your 'normal' surroundings, we recommend dressing or theming the room using posters and props. For example, a cardboard cut-out of a character that best sums up how you see the brand, as well as film posters and campaign material from brands that inspire you, or objects that might be in the life of your target audience.

The exercises fall into four sections. The first establishes the challenge and what it is you have to offer. The second drills down to the core of your motivations and gets your imagination going. In the third, those ideas are taken to generate a strategy, content and a look and feel. By stage four, you will have all the information to complete a genuinely inspiring creative brief.

KEEP AN OPEN MIND
THERE IS NO SUCH THING AS A BAD IDEA
YOUR IDEAS ARE AS VALID AS ANYONE'S
FREE YOUR SUBCONSCIOUS
LOSE FEAR

THE EXERCISES

1 Defining the challenge
– value proposition
– positioning

2 Freeing your imagination
– why are you doing this?
– your story and essence
– working with archetypes
– winning share-of-mind

3 Realising ideas
– creating a communication strategy
– developing content

4 Crafting communication
– the creative brief
– what happens next

DEFINING THE CHALLENGE

- Positioning
- Value proposition

"...the tendency that influences all of us to put more faith in information that agrees with what we already believe, and discount opinions and data that disagree with our beliefs"

The Confirmation Bias

Roger Dooley

Most people involved in marketing use these first two exercises. The challenge for creative people is that the results are often very formulaic and a bit dry. They rarely result in anything unique to work with in terms of a creative brief. The focus of these exercises should be to challenge the current perceptions and beliefs of a target audience. A great deal of marketing tends to be audience-centric (following the audience) rather than audience-leading. Building brands and leadership have a great deal in common.

Here we explain how to use a value proposition and positioning to form a solid foundation for a brief. We use value propositions to think through the real-world benefits for an audience and positioning to think specifically about who the audience are, what unique space they are operating in and how we can position the brand's best competitive feature, advantage and benefit.

By working hard to distil the real value and how this value might be positioned to excite our target audience, we stand the best chance of changing their beliefs.

VALUE PROPOSITION

This exercise aims to clearly define the value of what is on offer and at what price. In this instance, we are establishing a value proposition as a promise of value to be delivered – the primary reason a prospect should buy.

In a nutshell, it is a clear statement that explains how your product solves customers' problems or improves their situation (relevancy), delivers specific benefits (quantified value), tells the ideal customer why they should buy from you and not from the competition (unique differentiation).

①

②

Target audience	Benefit	Specifically, how? ideally facts and figures here	Rank 1–10 where 1 is most important
	Does the brand enable them to do something faster, saving them time?		
	Does the brand make them wealthier by saving them money or giving them something to sell?		
	Will they have less of a headache because the brand removed some hassle?		
	Will they be healthier because the brand improved their wellbeing?		
	Does the brand make them feel more empowered to help someone else or to do their own job better?		
	Does the brand reinforce a stronger sense of who they feel they are? (Difficult to put a value on this but we should still try to be specific)		

1 The brand's benefits

Great value propositions ascertain what benefit the brand has for the target audience. Does it enable them to:

- Do something faster, saving them time?
- Be wealthier by saving them money or giving them something to sell?
- Be healthier by improving their wellbeing?
- Have less of a headache by removing hassle?
- Feel better empowered to help someone else or to do their own job?
- Have a stronger sense of who they are, reinforcing their identity?

The most powerful of these benefits is the last – a reinforcement of identity – even though it is also the hardest to measure.

2 Facts and figures

The discipline of specifying some sort of fact or figure becomes more critical within the business-to-business environment when a higher degree of rational consideration means someone is more likely to stop and quantify the value of something.

A value proposition is an equation. We've covered the first part – the value you offer. The second part is the exchange and price: what is your price point and where does this place you in the market compared to the competition?

*WHAT VALUE
DO YOU OFFER?*

*The most powerful
benefit is reinforcing
someone's sense
of identity.*

Value proposition

POSITIONING

In this exercise, we define the target audience, the primary competitive feature, the advantage of this feature and its benefit compared to others that already exist in the market.

1 Who are you targeting?

Targeting is all about finding the early adopters or advocates, the people who can be relied upon to broadcast to a broader social or professional peer group. If the target audience is defined too broadly, then everything that we communicate also has to be as broad as possible. This ultimately makes a positioning too generic to be helpful when it comes to creating a brief.

The audience needs to be targeted as precisely as possible, and we need to believe they are the people who will broadcast the merits of the brand.

2 What insights do you have?

Insights are behaviour based and founded on findings. And the best results are borne out of research or experience.

An insight is a truth articulated in a new way – a leap of imagination. It results from immersing ourselves in the space and environment that the audience occupies, imagining their needs and how the brand could meet those needs in a new way.

3 What are you offering?

This should be short, simple, direct and to the point.

4 What is your primary competitive feature?

Technically what is different or unique in comparison to the current or other offerings.

5 What is the advantage of this feature?

The reason your target audience should believe in your offering more than what is currently offered.

6 What is the benefit of this advantage?

Theoretically, this is the same as the value proposition.

The task here is to spark the early adopters' or advocates' imaginations so that they will, in turn, fire the imaginations of the early majority. Once the early majority have bought in, the late majority, afraid of being left out, will buy in too.

Hey, everyone, you'll never guess what!

1. **For:** Define your early adopters
2. **Who:** What insight do you have – what is top of their minds?
3. **Brand X is:** Frame of reference – what is your service, product or organisation?
4. **That:** Point of difference – what is your primary feature
5. **Because:** Reason to believe – what is the primary advantage of this feature?
6. **So that:** Benefit – why do you think you can make a difference?

WHO DO WE TRUST MOST?

People will always trust friends, family and colleagues more than they will trust an organisation or a brand.

Positioning statement

2

FREEING YOUR IMAGINATION

– why are you doing this?
– your story and essence
– working with archetypes
– winning share-of-mind

"The world we live in is largely a manifestation of many individual and collective imaginations applied to the task of altering pre-existing reality"

Jeff VanderMeer

Having thought through the real-world benefits for a specific audience and how you want to position the brand, the following three exercises look at the motivations behind the brand and the audience. This will help the creatives come up with ideas and find the right tone and style.

Once we have explored motivations, we look at what the story could be, think about personality and begin to imagine how we can use these assets to win share-of-mind.

It takes imagination to create and communicate something meaningful to other people – which is a bit tricky because many of us, when growing up, were encouraged to focus on the functional stuff rather than use our imaginations. Reviving our imagination can be daunting. The good news is that there is stuff all around, which, if you let it, will trigger your imagination. The following three exercises encourage you to find those inspirations by asking you and your colleagues to be receptive, open and employ a large degree of spontaneity to the ideas that surface. Good luck!

WHY ARE YOU DOING THIS?

This exercise looks at the brand values and the beliefs that lie behind them; it looks at what you and the brand genuinely have in common with the target audience.

1 The brand's authenticity
This exercise will test how authentic the brand really is and is partially inspired by Simon Sinek and his organisation – Start with why (www.startwithwhy.com). Simon's ideas revolve around three central premises: Why do this?, How will it be done? and What will be done? These are very valuable considerations when trying to inspire the creatives reading your brief.

There are three layers to this authenticity:

a   **Values:** why are you driven to do this?*
What are the beliefs behind the brand?

b   **Style:** how will this brand behave in a way that is better and will make a difference?

c   **Function:** what is this brand doing that makes this an experience someone will want to repeat?

* Please do not answer by saying 'to make money'. It may be true, but let's face it, no one cares about anyone else wanting to make money. People only ever care if there is a benefit to them.

2 The target audience's motivations
Once these values are established, you will look at what you have in common with your target audience and ascertain what will resonate with them as a real motive. Material from the value proposition and positioning can be instrumental here.

Any audience targeted by a brand ultimately figures out what it is the people behind the brand believe in. Additionally, all markets these days are filled with people who passionately believe in what they are promoting. They have assertive sales material, dynamic websites and an evolving dialogue via social media. They also have significant representation at a sales level and customers who feel through the pores in their skin every detail and facet of the work put into building these brands. Many of these brands own their markets, so if you want to challenge them successfully, every promotional breath taken has to be authentic.

Brand building and storytelling are ultimately the same things. A good story resonates because it has a core truth that acts as a common thread throughout the story. A story has a purpose, a narrative and it is tailored to the audience (otherwise they stop listening). This tool views the story from three different perspectives to find the common resonant thread. Each aspect asks for a simple insight.

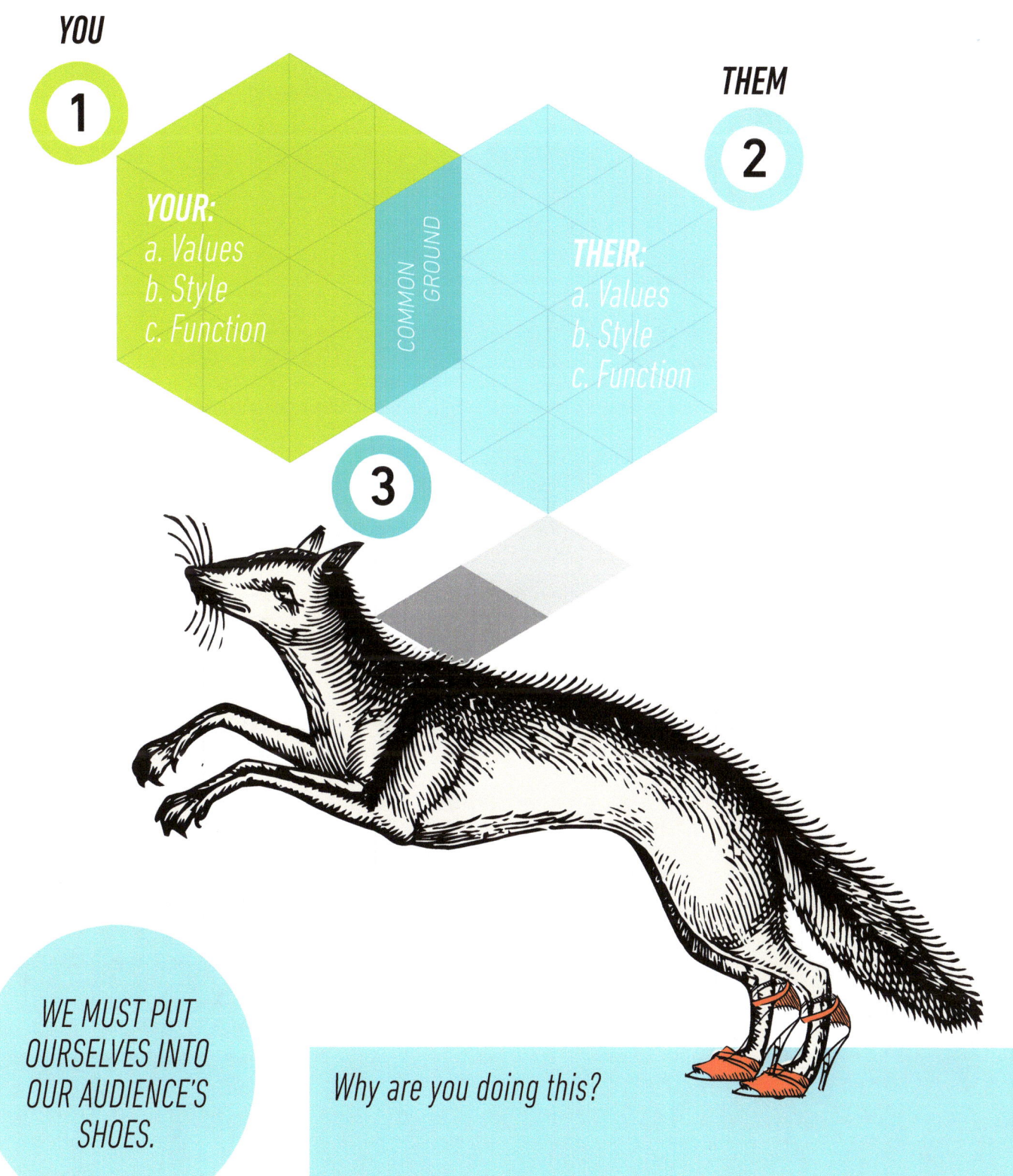

YOUR STORY AND ESSENCE

1 The ideal experience

The **promise** the brand can make within its marketplace:
What is the opportunity? How do you define the market
so that you can own it?

2 The subjective experience

The **perception** of the target audience:
their point-of-view – what is their unmet need?

3 The actual experience

Your **product, organisation or service's** primary features
and benefits by comparison to others:
What is tangible?

4 The brand essence

Where do these three perspectives overlap?
The shorter the essence, the better. You should be able to
explain its significance to other people quickly, and it should
fire their imagination. It should be inspiring.

All of the following aspects are critical to the story: the scene
in which the promise is made (the market), the perception of
the main characters (the target audience) and the action that
takes place (the product).

This process is most effective when the insights used come
from objective research. However, to carry this exercise
out successfully requires going beyond the findings and
employing some imagination, just as in storytelling.

The difference between insights and findings is not always
easy to pinpoint. However, there is a simple rule that helps:
an insight is an actionable opportunity.

INSIGHT OR FINDING?

The difference between insights and findings is not always easy to pinpoint. However, there is a simple rule that helps: an insight is an actionable opportunity.

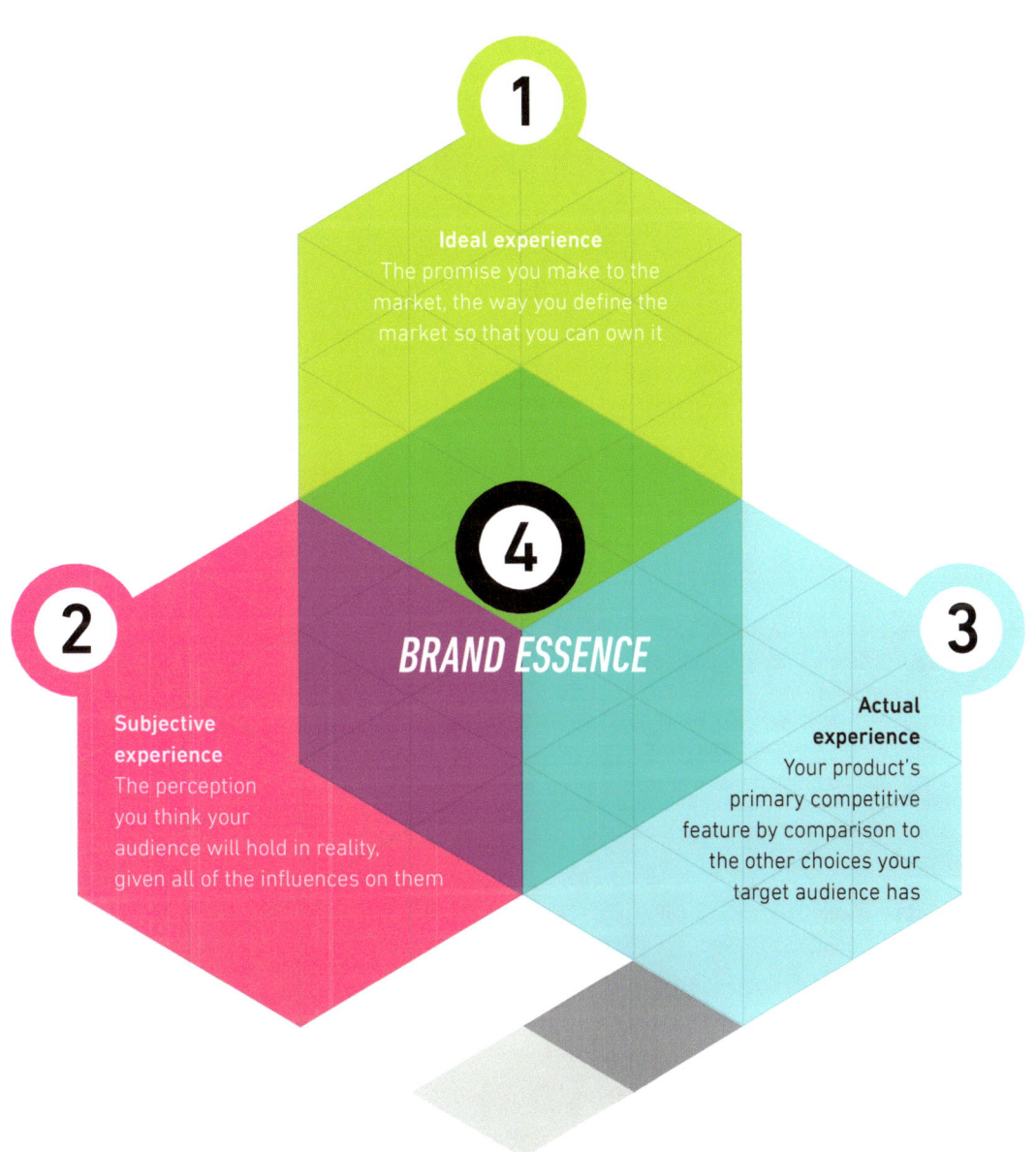

1

Ideal experience
The promise you make to the market, the way you define the market so that you can own it

2

Subjective experience
The perception you think your audience will hold in reality, given all of the influences on them

4

BRAND ESSENCE

3

Actual experience
Your product's primary competitive feature by comparison to the other choices your target audience has

Your story and essence

WORKING WITH ARCHETYPES

Assigning characteristics or a personality to an organisation or a brand is a good way of firing people's imaginations. These archetype models are used by those interested in behaviour and psychology, those interested in entertainment and by those with more business-focused goals.

Archetypes can be applied to organisations and brands. The process helps to define the story and behaviours in a way that people can relate to.

There are several of places you can start from:

If the brand is new, then it is perhaps better to start by reviewing which archetypes have done well in the marketplace.

It can be an interesting exercise to work out where you think the business is at the moment and where you would like to see the business in the future.

For example, messages from a warrior would be very different from those from an explorer. The imagery used for a nurturer would be very different from those used for an alchemist.

WHAT IS THE BRAND'S PERSONALITY?

Considering what type of personality a brand might have can be a valuable addition to a creative brief.

THOUGHT

ENERGY

Alchemist
TRANSFORMATION
clever
mysterious

Teacher
WISDOM
learning
enlightened

Entertainer
CREATION
fun
irreverent

Warrior
POWER
courageous
strong

Guardian
PROTECTION
champion
keeper

Patriarch
AUTHORITY
dignified
traditional

Explorer
SELF-DISCOVERY
independent
adventurous

Lover
ROMANCE
passionate
sensual

Companion
FRIENDSHIP
faithful
unselfish

Nurturer
ABUNDANCE
sheltering
tender

Artist
PLEASURE
alluring
mysterious

Innocent
PURITY
virtuous
selfless

SUBSTANCE

EMOTION

2. Freeing your imagination

WINNING SHARE-OF-MIND

This exercise helps you to imagine how a brand could win a share of the target audience's hectic mind.

Setting direction

To give the creative brief a strong direction, you need to ascertain how the brand intends to win attention, how it will engage, what its call to action will be and how to build up trust with the audience. It is ideas that count here. These ideas can take the form of messages, visuals or tactics or a combination of all three. It is a chance to take the theory from previous exercises and decide exactly what and how you want to communicate to the outside world. The four areas are:

1 Feelings/instincts

What will win the target audience's attention against the backdrop of a busy day and heavy media bombardment?

2 Rational/benefits

What claim or benefit can be made that will maintain that attention and achieve engagement?

3 Priorities

How will the target audience react, given the things they have top of mind?

4 Values/beliefs/mission

Why should they believe it's OK to trust your brand?

A campaign or a single piece of communication?

This exercise will differ depending on whether it is for a campaign or one specific piece of communication.

If the brief is being written for a campaign and you are thinking in terms of tactics, the share-of-mind wheel can be viewed as a journey with different media and tactics used to fulfil the four different criteria. For example, by developing something interactive like a game app for phones and tablets, you might win attention and generate curiosity. This will encourage players to follow a link, which leads to engaging information on a website with a clear call-to-action. They can then request further information by email. Slowly they become more involved with the brand as they learn to trust through experience.

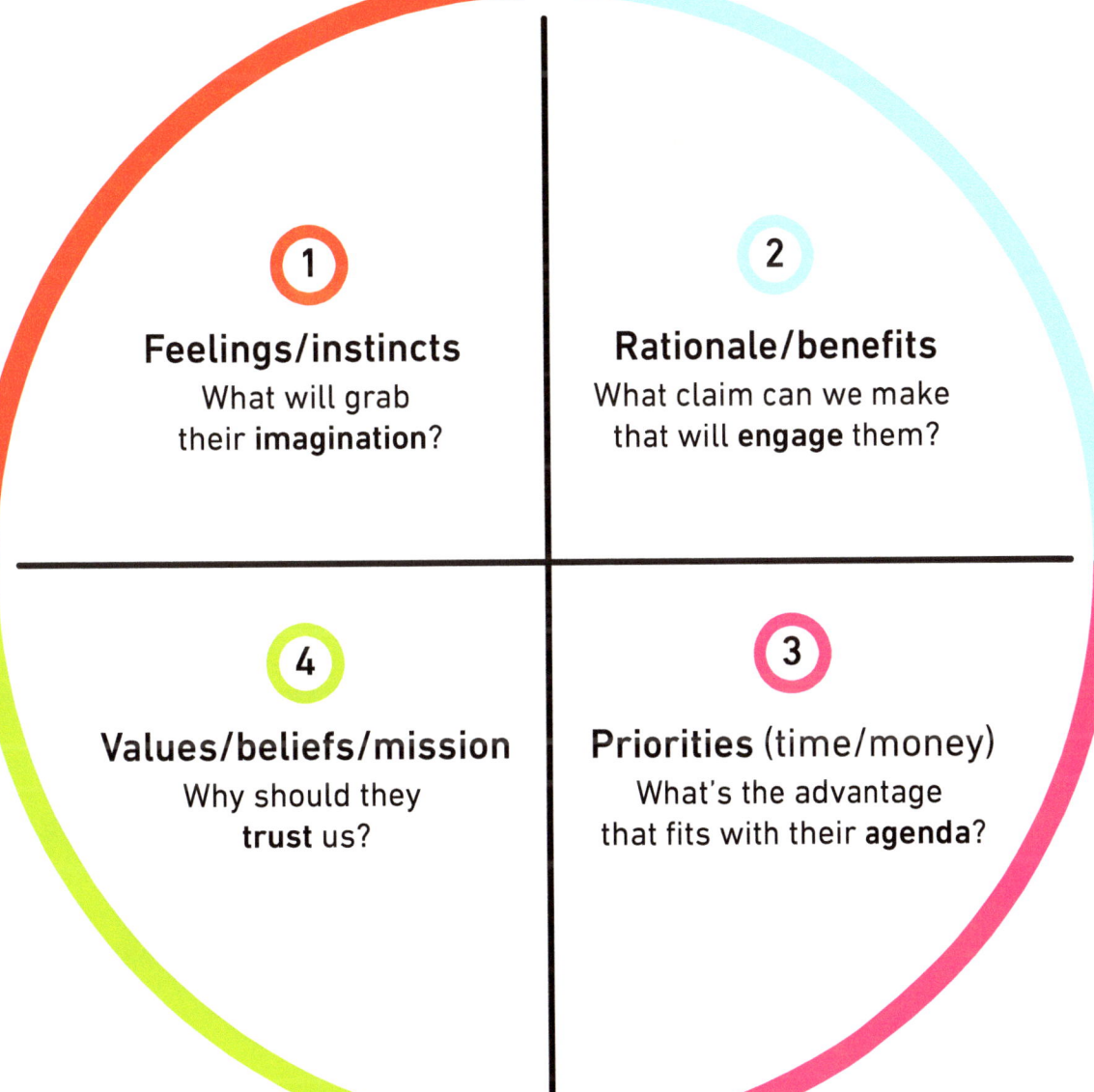

1

Feelings/instincts
What will grab
their **imagination**?

2

Rationale/benefits
What claim can we make
that will **engage** them?

4

Values/beliefs/mission
Why should they
trust us?

3

Priorities (time/money)
What's the advantage
that fits with their **agenda**?

Winning share-of-mind

3

REALISING IDEAS

– Creating a communication strategy
– Developing content

"Mine own eyes are not enough for me; I will see through those of others"

CS Lewis

If you have completed the previous exercises, you should have defined the challenge through a value proposition and positioning, developed ideas around the brand's authentic 'why', imagined the story and thought about the best way of winning a share of the target audience's mind.

The next step is to use these new assets, applying them within the structure of a communication strategy. Developing this strategy will enable us to determine the best tactics and develop the content for those tactics.

Pragmatic, actionable communication strategies are a challenge because there is a need to start with broad brush strokes and then drill down creating the detail. With this in mind, the following exercises start by assessing where the brand is now and where it should be in the future. This enables the appropriate key performance indicators to be put in place and determines what tactics are required to meet those performance indicators.

These tactics will then be populated with content, all of which should be driving towards what we call a single-net-impression, the articulated share-of-mind we want the target audience to hold of the brand.

CREATING A COMMUNICATION STRATEGY

This exercise translates ideas into a communication strategy: deciding what goals need to be achieved, through what initiatives and by what tactics. What will the new perception of the brand be as a consequence of the strategy? And how is that different from the current perception? During this exercise, you will think about tactics, the media, the channels and ultimately the measures that will determine the success of the strategy.

1 & 6 Today and tomorrow

Where is your brand today and where you would like it to be in the future as a result of the communication or campaign?

2 Strategy

A short description or title summarising the strategy which could include a significant fact or figure-based measure of success.

3 Goals

To achieve this future vision you need to define the key issues that have to be addressed to get there and set the goals that it is necessary to achieve to overcome them. The table below shows space for three goals, but there could be four, five or more. It is worth noting that the more you set out to tackle, then the broader the campaign or communication will need to be.

4 Tactics

Summarise in a single phrase the initiatives, channels and media that will be used to achieve the goals. Some imagination is needed here. For example, you might address the need for sales consultants to win more clients by equipping them with a web-based link to pass on to prospects. It might be a microsite with five succinct questions that persuades the prospects to communicate with head office and therefore helps the consultants avoid those awkward 'can we have more business?' conversations.

5 KPIs

Finally, what are the KPIs that are going to be used to measure the effectiveness of these tactics?

Media planners can vastly help with this task.

MEDIA HABITS AND
PATHS TO PURCHASE

Research (and a little
imagination) can identify a
target audience's media habits.
Finding out what these habits
are makes it easier to contact
the audience in the best way
and at the best time.

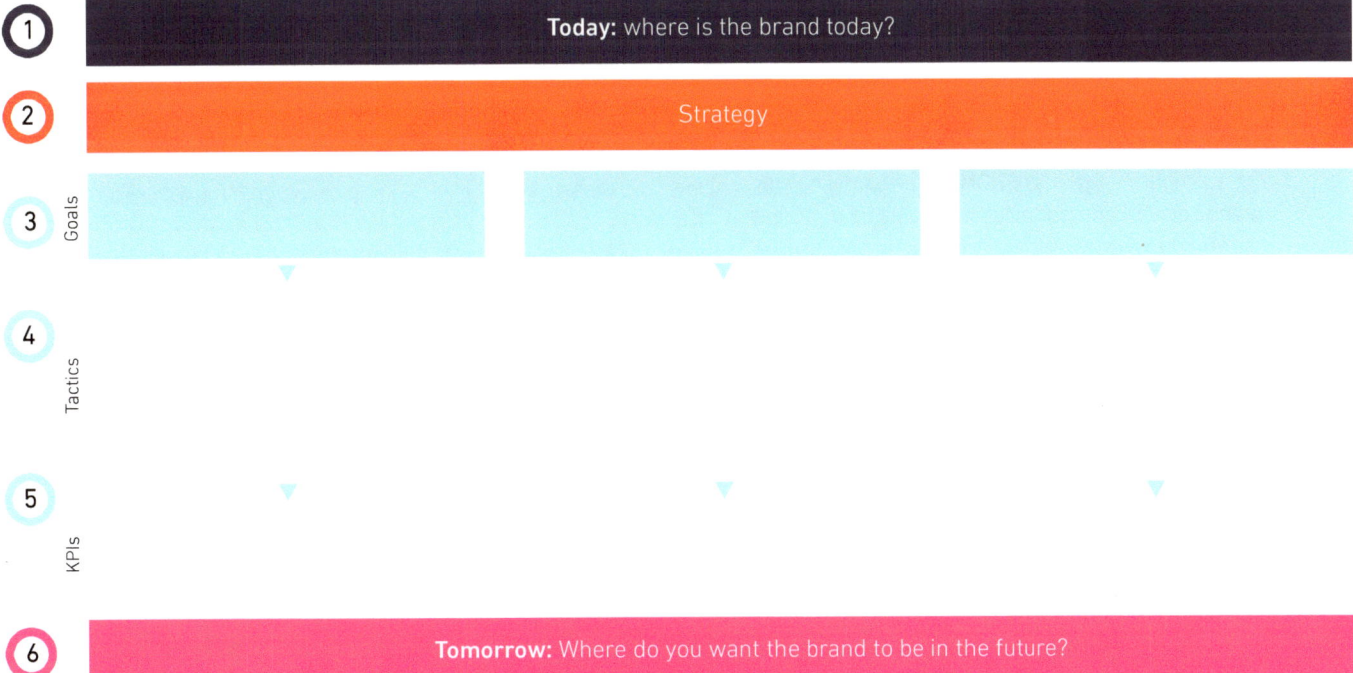

1 **Today:** where is the brand today?

2 Strategy

3 Goals

4 Tactics

5 KPIs

6 **Tomorrow:** Where do you want the brand to be in the future?

Creating a communication strategy

3. Realising ideas
CREATING A COMMUNICATION STRATEGY

Key performance indicators

These could include demonstrating an increase in market share, sales, awareness, recall or the penetration a brand has within a specific segment. Increasingly, marketers talk in terms of Return on Marketing Investment (ROMI) or Return on Marketing Objectives (ROMO).

Return on Marketing Investment

At a simple level, think of ROMI in the following way: X has been spent on the campaign and sales have increased by Y, so we have a return of Z on every pound spent. ROMI can, however, take a more complex form because it is not always easy to identify which specific activity or even external factor is making the difference to sales.

Return on Marketing Objectives

ROMO is focused on the objectives; building up awareness of X or perhaps changing the perception of Y. ROMO is sometimes easier to apply because not all campaigns are purely sales focused. Research may, for example, show that a brand is no longer perceived as innovative. Over the next six months, a campaign rolls out with specific audiences to demonstrate the brand's innovative qualities and then the research is repeated, demonstrating the Return on Marketing Objective. Researching before and after a campaign or initiative is always a good way to illustrate the difference it has made.

Measurement

It is not only how long they spend engaging with the media but what do customers do next? How does the digital media channel integrate with the other elements of the brand: forums, communities, the shop, the people or a service?

The best digital measurements are not those focused on the number of impressions, click-throughs or visitors, but the number of conversions or touchpoints achieved, or advocacy of someone who is telling their associates, family, colleagues and friends about the brand. 1% of an audience widely communicating its enthusiasm is much better than 100% of an audience paying the brand a single visit for a few seconds.

For example, campaigns are designed to make people curious, entice them to play a game, to encourage feedback, watch a movie, use an app or another inclusive tactic. In these cases, it is also the quality of their experience that has to be measured, and this requires intelligent interpretation.

So, the choice of media helps when trying to decide the type of KPI for a tactic.

The table opposite is not intended to be a comprehensive list of tactics, but an illustration of the sorts of KPIs that can be considered for some specific tactics. It is essential when viewing this list to think in terms of either pushing your brand onto your audience (e.g. advertising) or pulling your audience into a broader brand experience (relying on social media and more viral means).

Media	Measurement	KPI
Website	Unique users, page impressions, bounce rate, time on site, conversions	QT
Website with response form	Unique users, page impressions, bounce rate, time on site, conversions	QT and QL
Online video	Unique users, page impressions, views, view rate, watch time	QT
Social	Listening based research, engagement, actions, clicks	QT and QL
Apps	Engagement, actions	QT and QL
Games	Engagement, actions	QT and QL
Publication (print)	Circulation, readership, enquiries	QT and QL
Publication (online)	Unique users, page impressions, engagement	QT
Publication with feedback via letters/web/email etc	Circulation, readership, enquiries responses/views	QT and QL
Sales support material	Enquiries, sales	QT
Customer satisfaction via/e-survey/telephone	Responses and feedback	QT
Exhibition or event	Enquiries, sales, research of brand awareness (before/after)	QT and QL
Advertising (offline)	Enquiries, sales, research of brand awareness (before/after)	QT and QL
Advertising (display/online)	Clicks, CTR, conversions, website engagement	QT
Experiential	Enquiries, sales, video, research (before/after), behavioural study	QT and QL
QTEmail	Enquiries, sales, clicks, opens, website engagement	QT
Paid search	Enquiries, sales, clicks, CTR, conversions, website engagement	QT

DEVELOPING CONTENT

The call to action

When creating a communication strategy, it's important to think about exactly what you want the audience to do as a result of seeing your communication.

It's important to note that the call to action is not the same as the aim of the campaign. It may be that you are running the communication to sell more units but the call to action may be for the audience to visit your website or download an app. It may be that the action will lead them to purchasing something.

Media

It is imperative that the right media channels are used to reach the right target audience at the right time. With exposure to many media channels, and use of multiple devices, throughout the day, people seamlessly jump from one touchpoint to another, second, third screening or even fourth screening whilst consuming TV, for example. We call this the bumblebee effect.

It's important to capture the attention of your target audience during these micro-moments, periods of a few seconds in which people are consuming a specific media channel in the right psychological state to be open to receiving your message and achieving the campaign objectives and KPIs.

Who is your target audience? When and where do they consume media? What is their socio-demography, what age or gender are they? What are their interests and who do they follow on social media? Knowing this will help determine the most appropriate media to use, and the customer journey envisaged.

Each media channel has its own strengths across each stage of the customer journey: awareness, consideration, purchase, loyalty and advocacy. For instance, social can work extremely well in creating loyalty and engaging customers to drive advocacy. So we need to be aware of where media channels naturally sit in the customer journey and how each will benefit the campaign – then an integrated media plan can be created.

An integrated approach to the media strategy with a cross-channel methodology encompassing traditional and digital channels, driving traffic to a website to drive sales or creating awareness is often required. So don't just stick with one media channel, consider the customer journey and how each channel can integrate with another to achieve objectives.

Who do we trust most?

People will always trust friends, family and colleagues more than they will trust an organisation or a brand. That's why social media marketing is often an important element within an integrated media strategy. Even if someone doesn't know who they follow personally, they feel a connection with them through seeing their daily life. When those people then recommend things in brand partnerships, it's taken as a recommendation from a friend that you trust.

It is also worth remembering that however much equity a brand has, people will always trust friends, family members and colleagues a lot more than they will ever trust a commercial organisation or brand; hence the rise in social media influencers over the last decade.

Make sure the message fits the media

It is still the case that most visual communication fails to make the best use of the media available.

It's been more than 50 years since the term "the medium is the message" was first coined by Marshall McLuhan. Yet it still resonates today because understanding which media is best suited to which message is imperative if a campaign is to succeed.

If a reader can't find what they want in seconds, they quickly become frustrated. The problem is compounded by ever-increasing ways of receiving information and competing brands' ever-more sophisticated ways of pulling in their target audience.

Tone of voice

The tone of voice that you choose for your communications can make a big difference to the success of the campaign. It's important to consider both the target audience and also the brand's archetype. For example, a 'teacher' brand will talk to parents in a different way from an 'entertainer' brand talking to teenagers. The messages may be similar but the way they are portrayed will be different depending on the audience and the archetype.

What will the audience respond to?

What is appropriate based on the brand archetype?

How can messages be tailored to accommodate that?

Developing content

DEVELOPING CONTENT

Well-structured content is vital if you want to lead your audience through a proposition persuasively. This exercise is all about giving structure to the information, which can then be passed to a writer.

1 Single net impression

The single net impression is the impression you want the target audience to be left with once they have seen the piece of communication. Inspiration can be drawn from the brand essence (page 30), the overarching 'why' (page 28), or from the share-of-mind wheel (page 34).

Top level messages need to be prioritised with the single net impression in mind. Honing these messages is a difficult process and requires a lot of thought and time. This is where a writer can help immensely.

2 Pillars

Message pillars are the themes the messages fall beneath. They support the single net impression. The table below shows three pillars, but there can be more if required.

3 Top level messages

Headlines, subheads and breakers fall out of our pillars. At first glance, these are the messages the reader uses to gain a first impression of the relevance of the content to themselves.

4 Substantiating messages

Reference-able facts and figures (some of which will have cropped up in the value proposition and positioning). This information supports any claims being made at a top level – some of it may even make its way into the top level messaging.

1		Single net impression

2	Pillars			

3	Top level messages

4	Substantiating messages

Single net impression

CRAFTING COMMUNICATION

– The creative brief
– What happens next

"I find going to bed and pulling my imagination over my head often means waking up with a solution to a design problem. That state of limbo, the time between sleeping and waking, seems to allow ideas to somehow outflank the sentinels of common sense. That's when they can float to the surface."

Alan Fletcher

In this last section, you should be able to complete a truly imaginative creative brief, which is, of course our ultimate aim. We also talk a little about what happens next.

Engage early and be inclusive

The purpose of this book is to encourage the use of imagination when developing visual communication. There is a correlation between the inclusive nature of relationships within a team, the ideas that team produces and the effectiveness of that communication. Above all, it is a process that respects everyone's ideas. The more inclusive the process, the better the ideas. This is also true at the point when you engage a creative team. When you are choosing people to craft your communication, make your choices based on how inclusive the relationship will be. Whoever your team is going to include (depending on the output), we recommend that you involve them as early in the process as possible. The more involvement they have, the greater their understanding of your brand and your requirements.

You really need professionally trained creatives at this point. So, while there is a need to be inclusive when it comes to generating the brand platform, the direction and the core ideas for the brief, when it comes to the actual execution and crafting of your materials, specific training and experience really counts.

THE CREATIVE BRIEF

Creating the brief

In this final exercise, you take all the information, ideas and insights that you have collected in the earlier exercises and produce a creative brief (opposite) for the creative team, who will go on to produce the actual piece(s) of communication.

As well as this information, the following should also be included in the brief:

1 Other creative considerations

Any other creative considerations need to be taken into account here, such as any existing corporate guidelines.

2 How long and how much?

It is imperative that budgetary and time constraints feature on the briefing sheet. These details are vital since they will determine how ambitious the creative team can be in executional terms. In theory, time and money will not limit ideas (as long as there is sensible provision of both) but the theatre and scale of what can be done will inevitably be influenced.

3 Market situation and background

What is happening in the market and why do we see a business opportunity? Can we clearly articulate the business objective? What forces are at play that you'd like the creative team to consider?

RARING TO GO

Try to include the creative team in the project as early as possible to increase their understanding of both the brand and the project.

Title:	**Date:**
Project:	**Client:**

Value proposition How are you imparting value?	Time Wealth Hassle Wellbeing Empowering Identity
Positioning Primary competitive feature, the advantage of this feature, the benefit to the end user	**For** **Who** **Brand X is** **That** **Because** **So that**
Why you are doing this?	**Values:** **Style:** **Function:**
Story and essence	Promise (ideal experience) Perception (subjective experience) Product (actual experience)
Archetype	Can you attribute an archetype to your brand?
Winning a share-of-mind	We win attention by being ruthlessly emotive We gain engagement by making a logical claim We get action by analysing specific agendas We create belief by appealing to instincts
Communication strategy	Vision Strategy Goals and tactics Key performance indicators
Content	Single net impression Message pillars Top level and substantiating messages
(1) **The rules of any existing guidelines**	
Timeline	
(2) **Budget**	

WHAT HAPPENS NEXT?

Working with the brief

This book has been written to help you produce an imaginative, well-informed creative brief that inspires the creative team who in turn will produce work that will ignite the imagination of your target audience.

Only the best visual communication reaches its target

Once the creative team has begun, there is still a great deal to do. This is not something that is covered in this book, but the remaining stages are:

Creative and content development – it may take several stages to refine the content, the look and feel and the functionality.

Final crafting for client sign-off – a successful piece of communication can be assessed using these three questions:

- Does it inspire people to engage with it?
- Does it tell people directly how it might benefit them?
- Does it feel authentic so that people will trust whoever published it?

If the answer is yes to all of the above, then the creative brief was well thought out. Now, all you need to do is produce and distribute the final artwork.

Monitoring the measurables

The monitoring stage is as important as any other stage. Watching how a campaign or piece of communication performs informs the next step and the next phase of your campaign(s).

KISS

It's important to remember that whatever it is that you make, will almost certainly be viewed in isolation with no context. You can't presume that the audience already knows anything about your brand, product and the process you've been through to get where you are. Using an impartial person to view your campaign (someone who has no idea what it's about) is always a good exercise to see whether the communication makes sense without any explanation. Remember- you won't be stood over the shoulder of every member of your audience to explain it to them, they have to get it for themselves quickly and easily or they will move on.

What is good design?

Good design, whilst highly effective, is almost invisible. If someone is distracted by the fact that something has been 'designed', the 'design' isn't working as it should. Design should support the communication, not take centre stage. Using imagination does not mean adding unnecessary shadows, colours, boxes, it means inspiring as directly and truthfully as possible. Less is often more!

Below is a simple demonstration of this; there are two squares within squares, which inner square stands out the most?

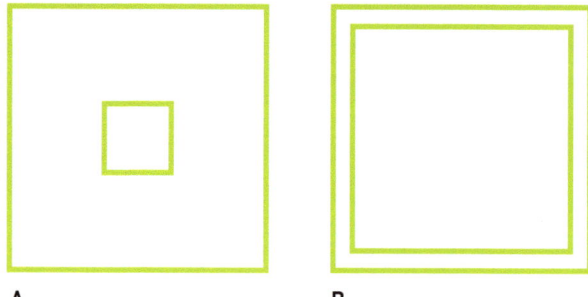

A   B

IMAGERY

COLOUR

TYPEFACE

LANGUAGE

LOGO

TONE

The answer is A. (If it isn't you are the odd person out! Research shows the smaller square is invariably seen to stand out more.) This is one of the founding principles of good design – the more space, the more effective the communication. The less you say, the more noticeable it is.

Identity

Put simply, a great identity is a lot more than a logo - it is a whole visual language of which the logo forms a small part. It is made up of colour, language, tone and imagery – every visual aspect of a brand. The target audience only sees the brand (and its identity) very occasionally, so if it is not distinctive and does not have elements that continually repeat, it is not doing its commercial job. Just putting the logo on every piece of visual communication is not sufficient either, because the logo is the trust mark. It is the stamp that sits in the corner with the authority of the corporation and consequently the people behind the brand.

Campaigns

Campaigns are an ever-changing and evolving part of an identity. They have a specific commercial purpose over a period of time. If a brand is well imagined, campaigns over the years should sit comfortably alongside one another with some sort of relationship in terms of the themes/ideas used, the execution, the personality portrayed and tone and style of language. Campaigns can be push- or pull-orientated and sometimes contain elements of both. However, as mentioned earlier in this book, these days a campaign has to earn attention and is perhaps best defined as being led by the target audience and their preferences rather than the desire to sell. A campaign has to find a way of adding value on its recipient's terms. As often as not, it is a journey where, at the outset, something is offered to the audience in return for them assessing their interest in the offering.

MORE THAN A LOGO

A logo is just a small part of a brand's identity. There are many other elements that contribute to its visual language.

SUMMARY

The brief is the bridge between the client, the strategist and the creative team. If the brief writing process and tools are used well, everyone has a stake in a better outcome, everyone feels inspired to do their best, everyone's expectations are surpassed and, of course, time, budget and energy are used more effectively.

At the outset, we said it takes imagination to create and communicate something that is meaningful to other people. As creative people ourselves, we've always found the more direct the collaboration between clients, strategists and the creative team, the more likely it is the resulting marketing and communication will be imaginative and meaningful.

We hope you get the opportunity to share the exercises in this book and that the resulting brief goes beyond everyone's expectations. We hope that when the creative team read your brief, their eyes light up and the resulting campaign takes your brand to the next level.

WHERE IT
ALL STARTED...

Back in 2014 before we wrote Forget the Box, we decided to find out how people felt about creative briefs. We conducted a survey amongst marketeers, writers, designers, art directors and other agency staff.

The results were shocking if not surprising and they spurred us on to write the book – 70% of creatives only expected to see an inspiring creative brief *once a year* at best.

Yet 59% of marketing and communication professionals that took part, put out a creative brief at least once every two to three months, with over half of those doing it at least once every two to three weeks. This would seem to indicate that most briefs do not get the creative team, whose work we're all dependent on, very excited.

Writing a brief is challenging, according to 63% of the people we canvassed.

A large majority (76% and 81%) felt that direct collaboration between the creative team and the brief-writer ensures better results.

We wanted to address this because, over the last 25 years, we believe we have discovered an enjoyable, collaborative process that leads to imaginative, creative brief writing – it's the under utilised bridge between client strategist and the creative team.

Take a look at the full results overleaf.

THE RESULTS...

CREATIVES

1 How often do you receive a brief that stimulates your imagination?

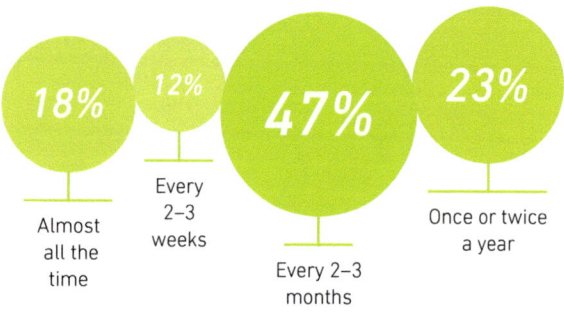

2 What difference does collaborating directly with the client make?

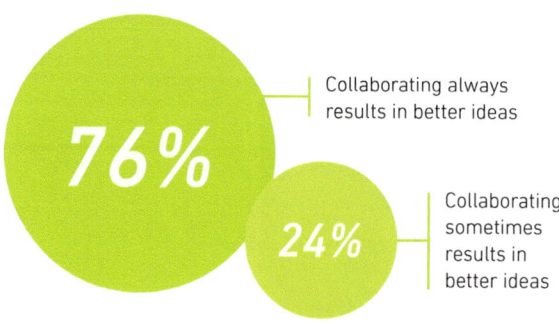

BRIEF-WRITERS

1 How often do you write a creative brief?

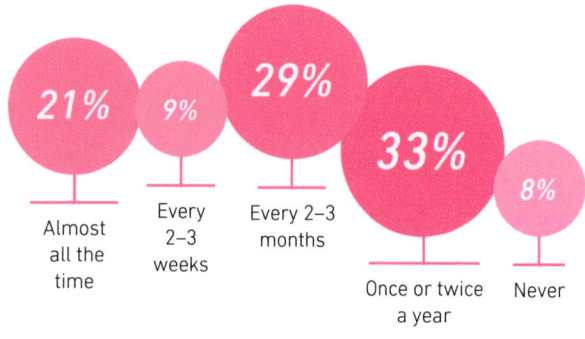

2 What difference does collaborating directly with the creative team make?

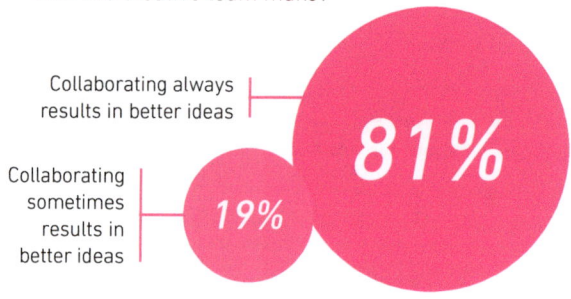

PURCHASERS

1 How often does your marketing or communications team send out a brief to a creative team?

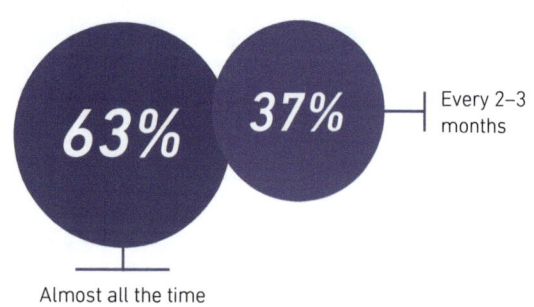

2 What difference does collaborating directly with the creative team make?

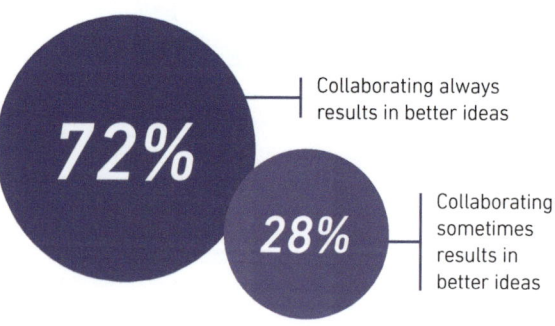

3 How important is a clearly structured brief in stimulating ideas?

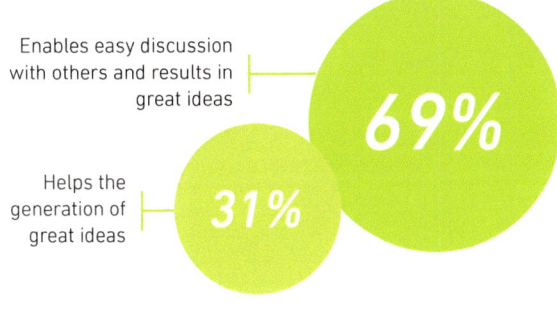

Enables easy discussion with others and results in great ideas — 69%

Helps the generation of great ideas — 31%

4 To what degree does the quality of the brief contribute to the imagination you can apply?

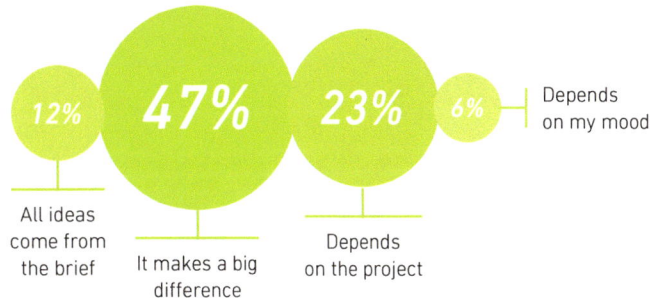

12% — All ideas come from the brief

47% — It makes a big difference

23% — Depends on the project

6% — Depends on my mood

3 How do you feel about writing a brief?

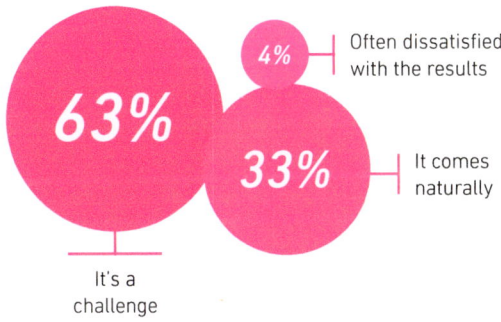

63% — It's a challenge

4% — Often dissatisfied with the results

33% — It comes naturally

4 To what degree does the quality of the brief contribute to the imagination the creative team apply?

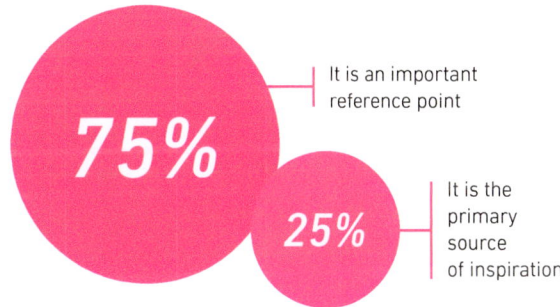

75% — It is an important reference point

25% — It is the primary source of inspiration

3 Which of the following most accurately describes your communications team's approach to formalising a brief?

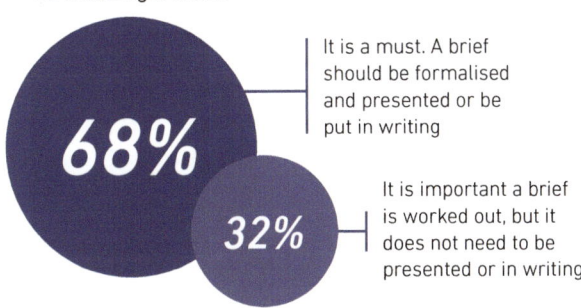

68% — It is a must. A brief should be formalised and presented or be put in writing

32% — It is important a brief is worked out, but it does not need to be presented or in writing

4 To what extent does the quality of the brief generated influence the effective use of budget and resources?

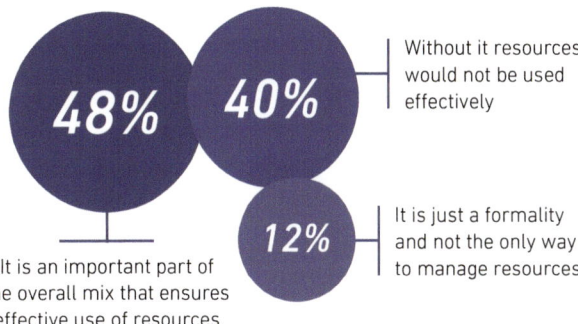

48% — It is an important part of the overall mix that ensures effective use of resources

40% — Without it resources would not be used effectively

12% — It is just a formality and not the only way to manage resources

ABOUT
KATE & STEPHEN

Stephen and Kate have many years' experience, having worked for, run and owned a number of well known agencies. Over the years, they have built up techniques, tools, processes and ideas to stimulate the imagination. In 2014 they formed Page & Page – an independent creative communications agency focused on creativity, brand, design and communication. They believe any creative process has to be inclusive, encouraging clients to work directly with the creative team.